A NOTE TO PARENTS

When your children are ready to "step into reading," giving them the right books—and lots of them—is as crucial as giving them the right food to eat. **Step into Reading Books** present exciting stories and information reinforced with lively, colorful illustrations that make learning to read fun, satisfying, and worthwhile. They are priced so that acquiring an entire library of them is affordable. And they are beginning readers with an important difference—they're written on four levels.

Step 1 Books, with their very large type and extremely simple vocabulary, have been created for the very youngest readers. **Step 2 Books** are both longer and slightly more difficult. **Step 3 Books,** written to mid-second-grade reading levels, are for the child who has acquired even greater reading skills. **Step 4 Books** offer exciting nonfiction for the increasingly proficient reader.

For Poppy, who started it all—S. A. K.

Photo credits: AP/Wide World Photos, p. 34; Bettmann, p. 36; Focus on Sports, cover (H. Aaron), p. 40; Foundation for the Tri-State Community, Inc., p. 44; National Baseball Library and Archive, Cooperstown, N.Y., cover, p. 10, 12, 19, 20, 22, 27, 28, 33, 39.

Library of Congress Cataloging-in-Publication Data
Kramer, Sydelle. Baseball's greatest hitters / by S. A. Kramer ; illustrated by Jim Campbell.
  p. cm.— (Step into reading. A step into sports step 4 book)
ISBN 0-679-85307-3 (trade) — ISBN 0-679-95307-8 (lib. bdg.)
1. Baseball players—United States—Biography—Juvenile literature. 2. Batting (Baseball)—Juvenile literature.
[1. Baseball players.] I. Campbell, Jim, 1942– ill. II. Title. III. Series: Step into reading.
Step 4 book. GV865.A1K73 1995 796.357—dc20 [B] 94-16497

Manufactured in the United States of America 10 9 8 7 6 5 4 3 2

STEP INTO READING is a trademark of Random House, Inc.

Step into Reading

BASEBALL'S GREATEST HITTERS

By S. A. Kramer

Illustrated by Jim Campbell

A Step 4 Book

Random House 🏠 New York

The Hardest Job in Sports

Batter up. The pitcher delivers. It's a fastball, steaming in at more than 90 miles per hour. The ball reaches the plate in less than half a second. The hitter must react in the blink of an eye. Should he swing? Is the pitch a strike or a ball? Will it hit him, causing serious injury?

To make the right decision, the batter must concentrate completely. After all, the bat must connect with an object only 2.868 inches wide. No wonder some feel hitting is the hardest job in sports.

Of course, great hitters do more than just get the bat on the ball. They swing with power and drive in run after run. When the game's on the line, they're the players who always come through.

There have been great hitters ever since baseball began. But in the early days the game was different. The ball was heavier, so it didn't carry very far. Pitchers could spit on it or scrape it, getting it wet and dirty. As the innings passed, the ball grew hard to see. Unlike today, the umpire didn't toss it from the field.

That time in baseball is known as the "Dead Ball Era." Hitters didn't clobber many homers because of the wet, dirty, heavy ball. But in 1920, teams began to use a light, clean, dry ball. A player named Babe Ruth started slamming home runs, and the game was changed forever. Now the greatest batters are usually sluggers. And fans love to argue about who's the best.

Keep in mind not all the top hitters played in the major leagues. Before 1947, African Americans were not allowed in the majors. Some of our most spectacular athletes were in the Negro leagues.

So, who are baseball's greatest hitters? Forget the fastest runners and the finest fielders. Not even the top all-around players count. This book is just about true heroes of the bat.

1

The Gentle Strongman

It's 1916, and late in the season. Forty-two-year-old Honus Wagner is coming to bat. He walks awkwardly, like a crab. It looks as though he can barely make it to the plate.

Honus has had a great career for the Pittsburgh Pirates. But he's about to face a tough rookie pitcher. Some fans are wondering, Can Honus still hit?

The rookie fires his best curveball and Honus takes a big swing. He whips the bat around so hard that he falls down on one knee. Honus has completely missed the ball.

The catcher is a rookie too. He and the pitcher are pleased. They think Honus can't hit a curveball anymore. They decide to throw him another. On the bench, Honus's teammate says, "Watch this next one."

The pitch comes in. Honus steps into it.

His knees bend a bit as he takes a full swing. *Smack!* The ball screams through the air into the outfield. It hits the left-field fence so hard, the fence wobbles for five minutes.

Honus has deliberately fooled the catcher and the pitcher. He missed the first pitch so they'd throw the same one again.

Honus was the most powerful batter of the Dead Ball Era. Some experts consider

him the best right-handed hitter ever. Yet Honus always seemed clumsy. His legs were short and very curved. His arms were so long, some joked he could tie his shoes without bending.

But this odd-looking man was one of baseball's most popular players. After games, he'd often teach children how to hit and field. He was so kind, he roomed with players nobody else would. He didn't care about money and never asked for a raise.

Honus felt lucky just to be out in the fresh air. When he was 12, he had had to work underground in Pennsylvania's coal mines. His family was poor and needed his pay of $3.50 a week.

But Honus's father encouraged him to play baseball. A scout heard how good he was and came to see him. He spotted Honus hurling chunks of coal against a train. He threw so well that the scout signed him up.

Honus went on to become a star. He was the first player to sign his bats. He was also

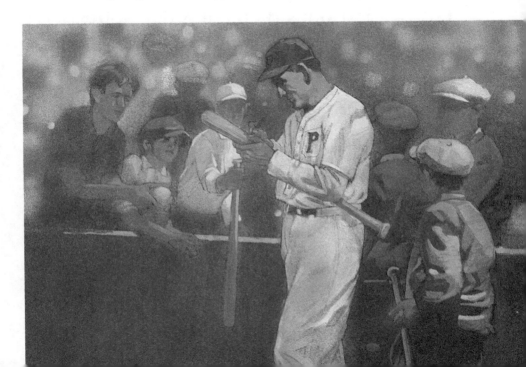

the only player to refuse to be on a baseball card. Back then, cards were sold with cigarettes, and Honus didn't approve of tobacco.

Honus played baseball nearly a hundred years ago. Yet experts agree he was the greatest shortstop ever. Some feel he is the most valuable player in baseball history. He still took batting practice when he became a coach in his fifties, and players stopped what they were doing to watch him swing the bat. They knew Honus was one of the best ever.

JOHN PETER (HONUS) WAGNER
(The Flying Dutchman)

1874–1955	Right-handed
5'11", 200 lbs.	Shortstop

Lifetime batting average: .327

Lifetime slugging average*: .466

Career: 1897–1917, mostly with the Pittsburgh Pirates

Hall of Fame

• Great Feats •

• Won eight batting titles, the most ever in the National League, and the most ever for a right-handed hitter.

• Batted .300 or better 15 years in a row, including .381 in 1900.

• Holds the National League record for most RBI titles—five.

• Finished in the top five for RBIs 14 times—more than any other player.

• Has the most hits of any man who played exclusively in the Dead Ball Era (3,415).

• Is third in triples (252).

• Is eighth in doubles (640).

• Is seventh in total hits (3,415).

• Is ninth in stolen bases (722).

• Greatest Feat •

• Struck out only 327 times out of 10,430 at-bats.

*Slugging average, or slugging percentage, measures a hitter's power. To figure it out, divide a hitter's total number of bases (single=1, double=2, triple=3, home run=4) by his number of at-bats.

2

The Man Who Had to
Be the Best

Detroit, 1912. Three men are trying to mug Tiger star Ty Cobb. But Ty battles back. He's not about to let himself be robbed.

Ty's a fighter, even when he's playing ball. He's been known to climb into the stands and slug a fan who's booed him. Once when he was heckled, he threw his bat into the seats. He shouts at umpires and spikes fielders guarding the bases. Many players think Ty is insane.

But now he is fighting for his life. One of the men has a knife. He stabs Ty in the back, and blood pours from the five-inch wound.

That just makes Ty angrier. He starts to punch fast and hard. Two of the men flee, but Ty chases the third down. He hits him so many times, he believes he's killed him.

Ty's own wound is serious, yet he refuses to see a doctor. Wearing a homemade bandage, he plays the next day. Blood soaks the dressing, but Ty slams a double and a triple. Not even a stabbing can stop him.

Ty would always do anything to succeed. "I've got to be first—in everything," he said. He didn't just slide into a base, he flew spikes-first at a fielder. Players knew he'd

try for the extra base, so they rushed their throws and made errors.

But it was pitchers who feared Ty the most. He did whatever he could think of to annoy them. On deck, he would grit his teeth, swinging three bats at a time. With his hooked nose and small eyes, he looked mean.

When he walked to the plate, he'd often

shout out an insult. Sometimes he'd bend over and shake his rear end at the pitcher. Once, at bat, he kept his back to the mound. The confused hurler fired four balls in a row.

Ty could hit any pitch, so no one was sure what to throw him. He always choked up on his short bat, hands apart on the handle. His knees bent slightly as he held the bat away from his body.

A tricky hitter, Ty did what no one expected. But he always made contact with the ball. Since he played mostly in the Dead Ball Era, he rarely belted homers. Still, he drove in run after run and was probably the best bunter ever.

By 1925, everyone wanted to be a slugger. That's when Ty pulled one of the greatest batting feats ever. He announced he would "for the first time...be deliberately going for home runs." To prove he could hit homers if he wanted to, he smacked three in one game and two in the next.

Ty performed feats few players could. His lifetime batting average is the highest in history: .367. Games were more exciting when he was in them—he'd get a single, steal second, and score on an infield out.

But Ty could be selfish. If he was in a slump, he'd stay on the bench to protect his average. When he didn't get his way, he threw terrible tantrums. Once he refused to play because he didn't like his hotel room.

Throughout his life, Ty had very few friends. He was prejudiced against African Americans and seemed more concerned about money than people. Even as an 18-year-old rookie, he couldn't get along with his teammates.

Baseball was the most important thing in his life. As a boy, he wanted to play so badly, he sewed his own glove and carved his own bat. Because his father disapproved, he wrote in secret to arrange tryouts. Once

in the majors, he worked hard to learn all he could about hitting.

By the time Ty grew old, he was bitter, lonely, and rich. Only three baseball people came to his funeral. Though unpopular to the end, he was still considered a legend. "To see him," one player said, "was to remember him forever."

TYRUS RAYMOND (TY) COBB
(The Georgia Peach)

1886–1961	Left-handed
6'1", 175 lbs.	Outfielder

Lifetime batting average: .367

Lifetime slugging average: .512

Career: 1905–1928, mostly with the Detroit Tigers

Hall of Fame

• Great Feats •

- Has the highest lifetime batting average.

- Has the second most lifetime hits (4,191).

- Is first in runs scored (2,246).

- Is second in triples (295) and fourth in doubles (724).

- Is fourth in stolen bases (891) and fifth in RBIs (1,937).

- Is fourth in total bases (5,854) and eighth in extra-base hits (1,136).

- Batted over .300 for 23 years (over .400 three times) and won 10 American League batting titles.

- Is seventh in on-base percentage—.433, with nine 200-hit seasons.

- Was the youngest to win a batting crown (he was 20 in 1907, and hit .350), and the youngest to ever get 1,000 hits.

• Greatest Feat •

- In 1911, he batted .420, with 127 RBIs, 147 runs scored, 248 hits, and 83 stolen bases—one of the greatest seasons ever.

3

The First Slugger

It's the third game of the 1932 World Series. The New York Yankees are in Chicago to face the Cubs. The score is tied in the top of the fifth inning when Yankee slugger Babe Ruth comes out on deck.

Babe is baseball's first power hitter. By clouting homer after homer, he has changed the game more than anyone else. But he's 37 now. Is he too old to hit anymore? Babe, however, still believes in himself.

Cub fans boo as Babe steps into the batter's box. Players on the Cub bench heckle him. When the first pitch is a strike, some shout "Baboon! Potbelly!" Babe, who is overweight, grins and raises one finger.

For years he's had trouble keeping himself in shape. He won't exercise like his teammates, or follow a diet. For breakfast he eats 18-egg omelets. Six hot dogs and six sodas make up a snack. At dinner he wolfs down two whole fried chickens.

The next two pitches are balls. But the third is a strike. The fans scream and yell. A Cub shouts: "You're just a tramp!"

Will Babe strike out? He does go after a lot of bad pitches. He never chokes up on the bat, and he always takes a big swing. He tries to sock the ball so hard that he sometimes spins around when he misses. But mostly he connects. Babe can homer on a pitch just above his shoes. He can whack a ball so low and hard, he fears one day he'll kill a pitcher.

Babe rubs some dirt on his hands. He looks at the Cub dugout and raises two fingers—he's down two strikes, but there's one left to go. Babe says aloud, "It only takes one to hit it." Some people think he points to the center-field bleachers.

Deep in the batter's box, Babe gets ready.

The pitcher fires. It's a change-up, low and away. Babe swings his heavy bat—the ball rockets into the sky. It goes over the center-field wall. Home run!

Babe circles the bases, laughing. "You lucky bum!" he says to himself. As he rounds third, he clasps his hands over his head. He ignores the garbage the fans are throwing on the field.

The Yankees win this game, and then the Series. Babe's at-bat becomes one of the most famous ever. His legend grows all the greater.

Yet even before that clout, Babe was the best-known American in the world. For years crowds followed him wherever he went. Stadium attendance tripled for games he played in.

Before Babe, a player could hit just 10 homers, yet lead the league. Then in 1919, Babe slammed 29. The rest of his team managed only four. This feat seemed even greater since Babe was best known as a pitcher.

In 1920, he became a full-time outfielder. That year he hammered 54 home runs. That wasn't just more than any other player—it was more than any American League *team*.

Yet when he was young, no one felt he would amount to much. By the age of eight, he was cutting classes, stealing, and chewing

tobacco. He had to be put in reform school.

Babe was always in trouble, but he was also generous and kind. In school he bought candy for the small boys and took the blame for their pranks. People didn't seem to notice

he was ugly—they just saw his joyful smile. After he became famous, he visited sick children in the hospital. Time after time he would leave $100 behind.

When he died at 53, the whole world mourned. No man was more a baseball hero than Babe.

GEORGE HERMAN (BABE) RUTH
(The Sultan of Swat, The Bambino)

1895–1948	Left-handed
6'2", 215 lbs.	Pitcher, outfielder

Lifetime batting average: .342

Lifetime slugging average: .690

Career: 1914–1935, mostly for the Boston Red Sox
and the New York Yankees

Hall of Fame

• Great Feats •

• First in lifetime slugging average, with the highest single-season slugging average (.847 in 1920).

• Was the greatest run-producer ever—drove in a run every 3.79 times at bat.

• Is first in home-run percentage (8.50). This means he hit more home runs in his number of times at bat than anyone else.

• In 1921, he had the most total bases (457) and the most extra-base hits (119) of any single season.

• Is first in total walks (2,056), with the most in a single season (170 in 1923).

• Has the second most homers in a single season (60 in 1927) and the second most runs scored (177 in 1921).

• Is second in runs (2,174, tied with Hank Aaron), homers (714), RBIs (2,213), and on-base percentage (.474).

• Is third in total extra-base hits (1,356), and fifth in total bases (5,793).

• Hit over 50 homers four times (more than anyone else), and batted .300 or better 17 times, including .393 in 1923.

• Greatest Feat •

• In 1921, he batted .378, with 59 homers, 171 RBIs, 177 runs scored, 44 doubles, 16 triples, 144 walks, 17 stolen bases, and a slugging average of .846—a display of power never equaled.

4

The Last .400 Hitter

September 28, 1941. The Boston Red Sox have come to Philadelphia to play the Athletics. There's a doubleheader scheduled, but the fans are interested in something else. They've come to watch Ted Williams bat.

Ted is only 23, but he's hitting .3995. More than anything, he wants to bat .400.

Today is the last day of the season. If he doesn't play, his average will be rounded up to .400. But he takes the field—he wants to prove he can really do it.

Ted has been feeling the pressure—his average has dropped 13 points in the last 12 games. Just last night, he walked 10 miles, worrying.

The Philadelphia crowd is rooting for the Red Sox slugger. Even some of the Athletics wish him luck. As he comes to the plate, the

umpire tells him to relax. But Ted is so nervous, his hands are shaking.

He steps into the batter's box and keeps his feet wide apart. Wiggling his hips and shoulders, he jiggles up and down. He swings his light bat and twists his strong hands around its handle. He's fussy about his bats—once he returns one because the handle is off just five thousandths of an inch.

Ted stares at the pitcher. He's concentrating completely. When the ball shoots in, he strides confidently forward. With perfect timing, he swings and connects.

It's a drive down the first-base line. The crowd hopes it's a hit. When it falls in for a single, they cheer Ted on.

Next time up he homers. Then he gets two more singles. He's batting .404 now, but still he won't sit down. He's going to play the whole doubleheader. He wants everyone to know he's truly a great hitter.

The fans roar each time he comes to the plate. He gets two more hits, one a line drive blasted so hard that it dents an outfield loudspeaker.

By the end of the day, Ted is batting .406. He finishes the season first in average,

homers, walks, runs scored, slugging average, and on-base percentage. All his years of
practice have finally paid off.

Ted has always "wanted to be the greatest hitter who ever lived." He started playing baseball when he was six. At the age of 12, he spent most nights in his backyard, practicing hitting in the moonlight. His parents didn't stop him. They were rarely around. Ted was lonely, underweight, and tense—but he loved swinging a bat.

By the time he was 20, Ted was in the majors. He studied pitchers and umpires, becoming an expert on the strike zone. He knew the slope of each stadium's batter's box and the direction of the wind. Like a scientist, he researched how the ball moves to the plate.

Ted was baseball's most patient hitter. He rarely swung at pitches that weren't strikes. But some say he thought only of his average and didn't care about his team.

Ted wasn't easy to get along with. He threw tantrum after tantrum. At the ball-park, he hurled bats, ripped out pipes, and smashed lights. He spat at fans who booed him. To show he didn't care what people thought, he never tipped his cap to a cheering crowd. When he homered in his very last time at bat, he wouldn't acknowledge the applause.

As rude as Ted was, he could also be generous. From childhood on, he helped the sick

and the needy. He raised millions of dollars for a children's cancer hospital.

Hitting, though, was what he cared about most of all. Many who saw him play insist he was the greatest of all time.

THEODORE SAMUEL (TED) WILLIAMS

(The Kid, The Splendid Splinter)

1918–   Left-handed

6'3", 205 lbs.   Outfielder

Lifetime batting average: .344

Lifetime slugging average: .634

Career: 1939–1960, with the Boston Red Sox

Hall of Fame

• Great Feats •

• Has the highest lifetime on-base percentage (.483) and the highest single-season percentage (.551 in 1941).

• Is the only American Leaguer to win two triple crowns (first in league in RBIs, homers, and batting)—1942 and 1947.

• At 21, he had what may be the greatest rookie year ever (.327, 31 homers, 145 RBIs).

• Is second in lifetime slugging average and in walks (2,019).

• Is sixth in lifetime batting average.

• Led the league in batting average seven times and slugging average nine times.

• Led the league in walks eight times.

• Is the oldest player ever to win a batting championship (he was 40 in 1958, and hit .328).

• Set many records despite serving five years in the Navy at the height of his career.

• Greatest Feat •

• The last .400 hitter, he hit .406 in 1941, with 37 homers, 120 RBIs, 135 runs scored, 145 walks, a slugging average of .735, and an on-base percentage of .551. He struck out only 27 times that season.

5

The Home-Run King

Atlanta, April 8, 1974. Hank Aaron slowly walks to the plate. A hush falls over the jam-packed stadium. Over 50,000 fans are at this Braves-Dodgers game. Right now they all have their eyes fixed on Hank. Is tonight the night he'll break Babe Ruth's home-run record?

Some white people don't want Hank to outhit Babe. Because Hank is black, they don't feel he's Babe's equal. They mail letters that threaten him and his family. The FBI is brought in to investigate. Hank gets protection from a police bodyguard.

This isn't the first time that baseball has placed Hank in danger. When he began his career, some felt that whites and blacks shouldn't play on the same team. White fans jeered him. Some threatened to shoot him.

White players called him terrible names. A few pitchers threw at him on purpose.

Their prejudice made Hank determined to succeed. He knew that the best way to show that blacks are equal was to play as well as he could. Controlling his anger, he kept swinging his bat. Because he was a quiet man, few fans noticed his achievements. But

tonight he can prove he's a great player. He'll make history for himself and for all blacks.

It's the fourth inning. Hank stands in the back of the batter's box. The Dodger pitcher knows he must be careful—Hank can hit almost anything. It's especially hard to throw a fastball by him.

The pitch sails in. It's a change of pace, in the dirt. Hank doesn't swing—he's waiting for the right pitch. As usual, he seems calm. But the tension is building. It's as if everybody's holding their breath.

The pitcher delivers, but he's made a mistake. It's a slider down the middle. Hank can wallop this ball!

With perfect timing, Hank waits till the last second. Then he shifts all his weight to his front foot. With quick wrists, he whips the bat around. Fans hear the wood smack the ball.

It's a line drive. For an instant, Hank thinks the shortstop can catch it. But the ball speeds high and deep to left-center field. It shines like a comet in the stadium lights.

Will the left-fielder catch it? No—it sails over the fence! Hank has hit home run number 715. The record is his.

The crowd explodes in cheers. Hank starts to circle the bases. He feels as if everything is happening in slow motion. The Dodger first baseman reaches out and shakes his hand. Two college students race from the stands and pat him on the back as he rounds second.

At home plate, all his teammates congratulate him. They try to lift him onto their shoulders, but Hank won't let them. He wants to embrace his parents, who have come out onto the field. Later he says, "I never knew that my mother could hug so tight."

Hank begins to cry. He's both happy and relieved. "Thank God it's over," he says after the game.

Hank Aaron holds baseball's record for the most home runs and most runs batted in. Yet the greatness he achieved came only after years of struggle.

Born poor in Alabama, Hank often had no money to buy baseballs. So he made his own by rolling stockings around golf balls. Sometimes he batted crumpled tin cans.

At 18 he became a professional player,

even though his mother wanted him to teach
school. He hit steadily and well, but few felt
he was a true power hitter. He never showed
emotion and didn't have a flashy style.
Despite his excellence, there always seemed
to be a bigger star.

But season after season, Hank produced
runs. It was his consistency as a hitter that
made him great. The record shows, as one
writer said, that Hank was "the man who
did the most with a baseball bat."

HENRY LOUIS (HANK) AARON
(Hammerin' Hank)

1934–	Right-handed
6', 180 lbs.	Outfielder

Lifetime batting average: .305

Lifetime slugging average: .555

Career: 1954–1976, mostly for the Milwaukee,

then the Atlanta, Braves.

Hall of Fame

• Great Feats •

• Is first in total homers (755), RBIs (2,297), total bases (6,856), and extra-base hits (1,477).

• Is third in total hits (3,771).

• Is second in runs scored (2,174, tied with Babe Ruth).

• Played in the third most games (3,298).

• Had 40 or more homers eight times.

• Had more than 100 RBIs 11 times.

• Hit .300 or better 14 times.

• Was the second youngest player to get 1,000 hits.

• Greatest Feat •

• Hank is one of only four players in history to get 3,000 hits, 300 homers, and 200 stolen bases.

6

More Greats

There are other players whom experts rank among the top hitters. Here are some in brief.

Joe Jackson (Shoeless Joe) has the third highest lifetime batting average ever: .356. A poor Southern boy, he couldn't read or write, but he would hit the ball so hard, one man said, "It could eat your hand off." He was banned from baseball after taking money to throw the 1919 World Series. When he left the court after his trial, a little boy cried out: "Say it ain't so, Joe." *Career:* 1908–1920.

Rogers Hornsby (Rajah) batted .424 in 1924—this century's highest batting average. The only National League player to win the triple crown twice, his career batting average is .358. Cold and insensitive, he was hated by other players, but some feel he was the best right-handed hitter ever. He was so hard to get out that one hurler said, "You pitched and you prayed." *Career:* 1915–1937.

Lou Gehrig (The Iron Horse) was known as the Pride of the Yankees. Scorned by his teammates as a mama's boy, he was sensitive and shy. Yet he hit balls so hard that one once smashed off a center-field beam and rebounded all the way to the infield. Third in career slugging (.632) and RBIs (1,995), Lou is best known for playing in the most consecutive games (2,130). He died at 37 of amyotrophic lateral sclerosis, now known as Lou Gehrig's disease. *Career:* 1923–1939.

Josh Gibson was called the black Babe Ruth. It's believed he smacked 75 homers in 1931 and batted .457 in 1936. A Negro leagues star, he was naturally strong. One man said he had "arms like sledgehammers." More than once, he hit a homer with one hand. He smashed balls so hard that one homer splintered an outfield seat. He died at 35 of a brain tumor. *Career:* 1930–1946.

Stan Musial (Stan the Man) was the most respected player of his day. For 16 straight years, he hit over .300. A perfect gentleman, he had a smile for everyone. His career proves nice guys don't finish last—he is second in total bases (6,134) and extra-base hits (1,377), and fourth in total hits (3,630). He won the National League batting crown seven times. *Career:* 1941–1963.

Willie Mays (The Say Hey Kid) may have been the greatest all-around player ever. His first hit was a homer, and he never stopped slugging. Third in total bases (6,066) and homers (660), he is fourth in extra-base hits (1,323). He had over 100 RBIs 10 times, and scored over 100 runs 12 times. Baseball was Willie's greatest love—legend has it he learned to walk at just six months by following a rolling baseball. *Career:* 1951–1973.